FLYING BACKBONE:
THE GEORGIA O'KEEFFE POEMS

by
Christopher Buckley

BLUE LIGHT PRESS
1st WORLD
PUBLISHING

FLYING BACKBONE:
THE GEORGIA O'KEEFFE POEMS
Copyright ©2008 by Christopher Buckley

1ST WORLD LIBRARY
PO Box 2211, Fairfield, Iowa 52556
www.1stworldlibrary.com

BLUE LIGHT PRESS
PO Box 642, Fairfield, Iowa 52556

AUTHOR
cbuckley@mail.ucr.edu

BOOK DESIGN
Melanie Gendron
www.melaniegendron.com

COVER ART
"Flying Backbone, 1944"
By Georgia O'Keeffe
oil on canvas 12 x 30 inches
Used by permission of the
Carl Von Vechten Gallery of Fine Arts
and Fisk University Galleries
at Fisk University, Nashville, TN

PHOTOGRAPH
Nadya Brown

FIRST EDITION

LCCN: 2007943706

ISBN: 978-1-4218-9848-3

CONTENTS:

Acknowledgements 6
Forward — The Artist First 8

I

Blossoms & Bones:
On the Life and Work of Georgia O'Keeffe—1988

1

Sky Above Clouds 22
Starlight Night 23
Red Poppy 24
Light Coming on the Plains 26
From 10 Variations on the Evening Star in Daylight
    (#s III, IV, V, VI) 27
Palo Duro Canyon 28
Dead Cottonwood Tree, Abiquiu, New Mexico, 1943 29
Train in the Desert 30

2

Summer Days/Ram's head with Hollyhock 31
Ladder to the Moon 33
Black Cross, New Mexico 34
Two Jimson Weeds 35
A Blackbird with Snow-covered Hills/Black Bird Series
    (In the Patio IX) 36
Black Hills and Cedar 37
Ansel Adams' Photo "Georgia O'Keeffe and Orville Cox,
    Canyon de Chelly National Monument 1937" 38

3

The New York Paintings 39
59th Street Studio 40
East River No. 1 41
Lake George with Crows/Black Hollyhock, Blue
    Larkspur/The Lawrence Tree 43
Pelvis and Moon/Pelvis III/Cow's Skull—Red, White
    and Blue 45

From the White Place 46
Road Past the View 47

4
Shell 1 48
Ranchos Church No. 1 49
Black Cross with Stars and Blue 50
Philippe Halsman's Photo of Georgia O'Keeffe at Abiquiu,
    New Mexico, 1948 51
Red Hills and the Sun, Lake George 53
Shell and Old Shingle VII (mountain across the lake) 54
Red Hills and Bones 55
Juan Hamilton's Black & White Photo on the Back of
    the Penguin Edition of the Paintings 56

II Against The Blue—2001

1
Spring, 1948 60
Red Hills with White Cloud 61
Blue River—Chama River, Ghost Ranch 62
Rust Red Hills 63
White Place in Shadow 65

2
Hills and Mesa to the West 66
Pelvis IV, (Oval with Moon) 67
Flying Backbone 69
Pelvis with the Distance 70
Hernandez Church, New Mexico 71

3
Black Place Painted Grey 72
Red Hills with Pedernal, White Clouds 73
Datura and Pedernal 74

Above Clouds Again   75
The Beyond (last unfinished painting)   76

III The Sudden Sky—2003

From the Plains   78
Pelvis with Shadows and the Moon   79
White Sweet Peas   80
Memory—Late Autumn   81
On the Old Santa Fe Road   82

IV 2007

From the Faraway Nearby   86
"That memory or dream thing I do..."— Pedernal,
    1945   88

V About Christopher Buckley   91

ACKNOWLEDGMENTS:

The Artist First—*The Montserrat Review*, No. 3

Blossoms & Bones
Two Jimson Weeds—*Antaeus*, Vol. 40/41
Dead Cottonwood Tree, Abiquiu, New Mexico, 1943;
    Ranchos Church No. 1; Red Hills and the Sun,
    Lake George—*Quarterly West*, #26
The New York Paintings; Palo Duro Canyon;
    59th Street Studio—*Ontario Review*, Spring 1982
Summer Days/Ram's Head with Hollyhock;
    Light Coming on the Plains; Red Poppy
    —*Nimrod*, Vol. 25, No. 1
Lake George with Crows/Black Hollyhock, Blue
    Larkspur/The Lawrence Tree; Ladder to the Moon;
    Juan Hamilton's Black & White Photo on the
    Penguin Edition of the Paintings
    —*The Chariton Review*
Road Past the View—*The New Jersey Poetry Journal*,
    Vol. 1, No. 2
Ansel Adams' Photo, 'Georgia O'Keeffe and Orville Cox,
    Canyon de Chelly National Monument, 1937';
    Shell and Old Shingle VII—*HUBBUB*, Vol. 3. No. 2
Black Hills and Cedar; Red Hills and Bones;
    From the White Place; East River No. 1
    —*Pacific Review*, Fall 1988
Sky Above Clouds; Starlight Night
    —*Cumberland Poetry Review*, Vol. II, No. 1
Train in the Desert—*The Bloomsbury Review*,
    Summer 1988
Black Cross, New Mexico; A Black Bird with Snow-
    Covered Hills/Black Bird Series (in the Patio IX);
    Pelvis and Moon/Pelvis III/Cow's Skull—Red,
    White and Blue—*Bluefish*, Vol. II, No. 3-4
Shell I—*The Sewanee Review*, Vol. 90, No. 1
Phillippe Halsman's Photo of Georgia O'Keeffe at
    Abiquiu, New Mexico, 1948—*Helix*, No. 16

Black Cross with Stars and Blue—*Quarry West*, No. 17

Against The Blue
Pelvis IV, (Oval With Moon); Spring, 1948;
    The Beyond (last unfinished painting)
    —*The Montserrat Review* &
    —*Still Light*—Sutton Hoo Press
Pelvis With The Distance—*Rattle*
Blue River-Chama River, Ghost Ranch;
    Red Hills with Pedernal, White Clouds Hernandez
    Church, New Mexico—*Wilshire Review*
White Place In Shadow; Black Place Painted Grey
    —*Art/Life*
Red Hills with White Cloud; Flying Backbone;
    Above Clouds Again; Datura and Pedernal;
    Hills and Mesa to the West
    —*Into the Teeth of the Wind*, Vol. II, No. 1
Rust Red Hills—*HUBBUB*

The Sudden Sky
Into the Teeth of the Wind —SOLO —*HUBBUB*

2007
From the Faraway Nearby —*Willow Springs*
"That memory or dream thing I do..." —*HUBBUB*

Thanks to:
The Poetry Society of America for the 1987
    Gertrude B. Claytor Memorial Award for
    "East River No. 1"
University of California Riverside for an Academic
    Senate Grant which helped support the
    publication of this book.
Vanderbilt Univ. Press for *Blossoms & Bones:*
    On the Life and Work of Georgia O'Keeffe
Blue Light Press for *Against The Blue*
Cutaway Books/Sutton Hoo Press for
    The Sudden Sky

Forward

The Artist First

I began to look at the work of Georgia O'Keeffe at the end of 1974 during my first year in the writing program at the University of California, Irvine. I was attracted to her use of light, her very direct celebration of the world in its elemental parts. Subconsciously at least, I think the bones, trees, flowers and hills among all that air and light—the cherishing of life that was implied in the paintings—appealed to some vision I had of the world that I had not as yet fully articulated to myself. I had no plan to write anything about O'Keeffe or her work, and for the next year or so her images and whatever themes I may have perceived just rolled around in the back of my mind.

I had, however, also been studying art and art history. I took many classes from Phil Leider, who is one of the best teachers of any subject I ever had. Classes I took from Leider were not focused on contemporary work, but he taught us how to look at painting. Neither Art Historian nor Art Critic, (he had been editor of *Artforum* for a number of years in New York and in San Francisco), Leider gave us both lines of thinking on a particular painting or artist and then supplied a view that often discarded both theories and considered, in a very immediate, specific, and practical fashion, the artist and the aspects of the work itself. He taught us to always "trust the artist first." After studying with Leider, consciously or unconsciously, I had a fair idea about how to look at painting.

In 1976, Penguin/Viking published a book of her paintings and her writing about her paintings, *Georgia O'Keeffe*. I spent a good deal of my free time looking at reproductions of her work and re-reading her own thoughts about it. I was fortunate to see a dozen or so paintings first hand in various museums. After a while, her voice/vision began to seep into my mind, into that place that makes and orders images, that finds words, phrases and lines for them. There was an elemental correspondence between O'Keeffe's images and a view I sometimes had of the world, and I began to think about a poem that might take up, tangentially, her ideas and vision. I had by that time written a handful of poems on other paintings/painters and so had some notions about ways to approach the subject. For two summers running I promised myself I'd take a block of time, sit down and work on a sequence of poems. But I was teaching part time all of the time, summers included, and that block of time never appeared. I did not even make notes—ideas just floated around in my mind like driftwood on an inland sea. Finally, in the summer of 1979, after I had moved to Fresno, I had two weeks free before the fall semester began and I sat down to work. In draft form, eleven poems came in a flash, like a dam breaking.

A couple of weeks later, two more poems worked their way to the surface; I was working mainly from the 1976 Viking/Penguin book which was really the first one to offer a significant group of reproductions and writing about her work. Soon, I had a group of thirteen, all written as monologues, as if O'Keeffe herself were speaking, and luckily I was so enthusiastic about her work that it did not occur to me that this strategy might be monumentally presumptuous.

I had written poems before as a monologues, as the artist speaking, but always with some conscious choosing and maneuvering. These poems on O'Keeffe's paintings just happened this way. From first to last, the poems came out of my mind and typewriter as monologues, and I never questioned them or the voice I heard in my head. The poems I wrote on her paintings, and on a famous photograph or two of her, were in fact not much like anything I had done before; they were shorter, more concentrated and imagistic. The rough drafts came in a rush, often two a day, sometimes three. I accepted the sound and the phrasing when it arrived. A little mystical, yes—but really, I was just so soaked in, absorbed with O'Keeffe, her world and voice, that the process was entirely natural. A voice had entered me and this was how it spoke.

O'Keeffe and her work were speaking, I was speaking, something was singing reasonably through me. If I had only learned one thing in graduate school—something I taught myself—it was not to question the style, genre, or theory of a poem or poems while they were being written. If work proved unworthy, it was no problem to discard it, to not publish it—I had good poet friends to trust on that count—but wearing the critic's hat, the theorist's long gown while in the midst of creating the work was a sure way, in my experience, to write nothing, or write nothing worth while. Finally, I had to take the risk that a reader would be compelled by the voice of the poems, would find it credible and would enter the vision of the poem and painting. Finally, it seemed more stilted and artificial to describe her work from a distance. The last thing I wanted was for the poems to sound like an art history lecture. The monologues worked for me and close poet friends who read my work, and I had little trouble publishing the poems in journals.

O'Keeffe was alive when I was writing most of the poems. In 1980, after I moved back to Santa Barbara, I sent out a manuscript, of thirteen poems to a small, letterpress publisher in Minnesota who accepted it. Each year thereafter, when the chapbook was not published due to a new excuse, I added a poem or two as I encountered paintings I had not seen before or ones I had looked at but not really "seen." After the initial burst, I wrote another ten poems over the next six years. By the time I moved to Pennsylvania in 1987 the manuscript was close to book length.

I traveled to Washington D.C. to see the retrospective show, and seeing that much work first-hand provided new energy and ideas. I wrote another handful of poems that seemed to complete the book, writing the last five or six poems, which brought the book up to thirty, after O'Keeffe's death. I withdrew it from the small press, figuring seven years was enough time to do something if they really intended to, and then submitted the complete manuscript to Vanderbilt University Press, which had published my fourth collection of poems. They accepted it, and *Blossoms & Bones: On the Life & Work of Georgia O'Keeffe* was published in 1988. The first printing sold out in nine months, and so it was lucky for me that the small press never acted. I did not flatter myself too much, however. O'Keeffe was so popular in the late '80s (and still into the '90s) that I used to say that you could sell sand in a can so long as her name was on it. I suspected that there were people who, buying a copy of my book with its beautiful reproduction of O'Keeffe's "Cow's Skull with Calico Roses" on the cover, were surprised to find poems inside instead of more reproductions of her art when they got home. My concern then was that I not look like someone trying to "cash in" on O'Keeffe's recent popularity—by this time, I had been working on my modest project for ten years.

I have a preface, a disclaimer really, in the beginning of that book which explained my methods and concerns; here is the salient part of it :

This collection of poems is homage, not homily. I am not attempting to speak for Georgia O'Keeffe, nor am I trying to define her work in any absolute academic or aesthetic way. In my opinion, too many have made that mistake over the years.

These poems are written as monologues, and in that sense they do assume O'Keeffe's voice.... I found this the most natural way to write the poems. It would be going too far to say that O'Keeffe's actual voice, the texture and vision of her life and work, entered my conscious or subconscious mind as I wrote. But I do not think that a person can spend a long time looking at her art and thinking about it and not be, to some degree, favorably influenced by how she saw the world, how she phrased her perception in art or in words . . . .

The monologue seemed the only "true" way to write, a risky way to be sure, but the only one in which the poems held immediate power and range and a chance of not sounding pretentious and academic. During the 1970s, poems derived from famous art were very much in vogue and many poets simply showed off their art history acumen. I wanted to avoid that kind of poem whose slim virtues resided only in esoteric information and detail. I wanted a truly human poem grounded in an accessible visual and thoughtful landscape, one that would balance the bright and concentrated images that jumped from the paintings on to the page with ideas and invention, while still retaining fidelity to the subject. (The titles of the poems derive directly from O'Keeffe's paintings: two or more paintings grouped together are separated by a slash (/). The three poems based on photographs carry the photographic titles.)

The poems were persona poems and thus contained more authority, and hence, latitude for my speculations about her work. I tried to bring the emotional, conceptual center of the poems to a resolution that was not only true to my own feelings but true as well to O'Keeffe's avowed ideas and her painterly details and focus. Although whatever I have said using this poetic device, is finally only my own take on O'Keeffe's images, I hope the affinity I felt with her view of the world was close and accurate enough to do her no great disservice.

Her paintings celebrate life—a life made beautiful not only by individual fortitudes, but by its wonder and uncertainty as well as by its shining reductions. She found vitality in everything from desert bones to skyscrapers in New York. She had a practical cast, one that found value in the earth and praised the strength of the natural, the human spirit as it endured. I wrote my poems doing the best I could to continue to see what she was showing us, using my own words to say what the images, in part, might add up to.

My poems then, were about her life and her paintings, her take on the world as I saw it and read it. The more I read about O'Keeffe in articles, in her letters, and in biographies—the more I looked at her work—the more I found I shared her responses. In 1985, Crown Books published *The Art & Life of Georgia O'Keeffe*, by Jan Garden Castro, which was a mix of reproductions of well known and lesser known paintings, photographs, and a critical monograph by Castro. I especially agreed with Castro's conclusions that O'Keeffe was, in a secular sense, a "spiritual" painter. Castro (*The Art & Life of Georgia O'Keeffe*, p.170) frames her view with reference to Mircea Eliade, author of *The Sacred and The Profane*: "The Sacredness to time, space and nature is a belief that distinguishes religious from nonreligious humankind . . ." Castro goes on to conclude a few sentences later that, "In some respects, O'Keeffe seems to fit the role of the sacred, rather than the secular, artist/creator. "Her works seem to exist in a universal present time . . . composed of a small number of forms with a ritual significance that inhabit a consecrated space." Castro is reasonable and accurate in her evaluation here because she largely appraises O'Keeffe outside of any orthodox or parochial theories—she is not out to "prove" that she has some special or discrete way to interpret the paintings. Rather, she is looking at a cumulative effect of the work and O'Keeffe's overall vision. In enunciating a "spiritual" cast to the work in general, Castro does not for a second ascribe that view, that texture, to any ideology, or *a priori* concept on the part of O'Keeffe.

Castro goes on to ask, "Why does O'Keeffe deny the male and female symbols in her work? This issue . . . seems to involve O'Keeffe's determination to assert the real, as opposed to the symbolic, nature of each object. Nor did she favor the religious interpretation of the earth as a sign of fertility, a bearer of life and death. Her opinion about the significance of dreams is unknown." Castro correctly, I believe, realizes that O'Keeffe's concerns, first, last and always, were formal, painterly concerns, just as O'Keeffe said all along. Her emphasis on light—within her objects as well as without—proclaims some essential vitality, some life principle that perhaps outlives death or transcends it. About the bones and skulls she collected and painted, O'Keeffe said that they had nothing to do with death, they outlasted it. Certainly for her, these were not symbols of death or mortality. If anything, they were only emblems of the landscape she loved, one brimming with elements that spoke to her about what it was to be alive in that space and to make art there. As anyone familiar with O'Keeffe's own writing and with painters in general will know, her subjects were chosen for their formal an essential qualities of line, tone, and space, and not for some "message" value. This is of course disappointing to the critics and art historians, the recently arrived deconstructionists and New Historicists whose business relies often on ignoring the artist in favor of their own manufactured concepts.

And this brings me to the problems, past and present, of interpretations of O'Keeffe's work. I hope my own poems are close to the views—transcendent in a general sense—of O'Keeffe. In writing a poem on a painting, a group of paintings, or on a photograph, I attempted to deal directly, factually, with the details presented in the work. But, I also let myself be guided by O'Keeffe's sensibility and aesthetics as she expressed them in her writing and as they were reinforced and amplified in the paintings. O'Keeffe's mind and vision are both speculative and determined, while most of the criticism of her work in the 1920s and '30s is arrogant and pretentious, and that line of response—the sexual, quasi-Freudian interpretation of the paintings offered mainly by men—persists into the late '80s and early '90s despite feminist theory and women writing the contemporary responses. O'Keeffe disavowed it directly and sensibly at the same time. Since then, comprehensive and intelligent essays by Jack Cowart, Juan Hamilton, and Sarah Greenough, published in the Catalogue for O'Keeffe's traveling retrospective show 1987-1989, *Georgia O'Keeffe: Art and Letters*, (National Gallery of Art, Washington] Little, Brown and Co., Inc., 1987)—have also pointed out the failings of these three interpretations. And, interestingly enough for our times, the sexist nature of the early criticism is there brought to light. Moreover, in this book, in letter after letter, O'Keeffe explains and reinforces her painterly priorities.

O'Keeffe was interested in things, but was also interested in their relation to whatever force they might have in common. She was sure about what engaged her as a subject for paintings, sure about the shapes in her mind for which she sought the exact colors. She was not an ideologist. She was open to discovery; she set out to make art in order to discover something, and that might be the relationships of color, line, shape, light or life-force. This approach is often true for artists—they have their antennae, their satellite dish, trained to receive information, while certain art critics or art historians who have already figured "it" out, are out to prove something.

The Penguin book also quotes O'Keeffe's writing about her interest in objects for painting and her practical approach. In talking about the first avocado (alligator pear) she ever had, she relates that she did not eat it but kept it so long it turned a light brown color: "I kept if for years—a dry thing, a wonderful shape." She continues, talking about painting two green alligator pears and that leads into comments on her views of art and criticism and the times, the early 1920s.

It was in the time when the men didn't think much of what I was doing. They were all discussing Cézanne with long involved remarks about the "plastic quality" of his form and color. I was an outsider, My color and form were not acceptable. It had nothing to do with Cézanne or anyone else. I didn't understand what they were talking about—why one color was better than another. I never did understand what they meant by "plastic." Years later when I finally got to Cézanne's Mont Sainte-Victoire in the south of France, I remember sitting there thinking, 'How could they attach all those analytical remarks to anything he did with that mountain?" All those words piled on top of that poor little mountain seemed too much.

The 1976 Penguin/Viking edition of O'Keeffe's paintings and writing about painting is very helpful, for while O'Keeffe wrote a little about her work to friends in letters and for herself in memoirs, she did not comment publicly about her own work. And so that book offers many good sentences by O'Keeffe which address her intentions clearly and directly, and which, if one bothers to study the letters and biographies, seems to be the way she approached most her life and her art. Wonder, the speculative nature of life and the earth as she saw it, was important to O'Keeffe's vision—she was not simply a maker of icons.

She said, "I have used these things (flowers and bones) to say what is to me the wideness and wonder of the world as I live in it." In the same book she says, "The unexplainable thing in nature that makes me feel the world is big far beyond my understanding—to understand maybe by trying to put it into form. To find the feeling of infinity on the horizon line or just over the next hill."

Perhaps her work can be seen as asking a question about transcendence, posing some possibility about the subject. Jan Garden Castro points out that she cherishes life in her attention to the elements of her environment, to the time and space around her. Yet this is very subtle in the work; what is clear is that at the heart of her considerations are the questions of a painter's composition, of form—the same questions which must be answered whether one paints representationally or abstractly. "It is surprising to me," O'Keeffe said early on, "to see how many people separate the objective from the abstract." Much of her flower series paintings works toward abstraction. The Jack in the Pulpit series is a good example; Numbers IV, V and VI move up closer and closer to the flower until, in the end, lines and colors are in fact abstractions and the obvious focus becomes two-dimensional. O'Keeffe looked for correspondences of color and line, and regularly developed formal themes found in representative subjects into non-representational compositions.

Of course, there are many of her paintings that simply are abstract. The series "Shell and Old Shingle," which begins with clamshells and a roof shingle, works into abstraction by number IV and into another complete correspondence in number VIII—a painting in which O'Keeffe paints the mountain across a lake. The Blackbird series works in much the same way, the lines of the bird being reduced and simplified until the mark-making then is not about representation but about shape and space. There are many other examples throughout her work. Her flowers were expanded for their abstract qualities and to make people notice them. Responding to some early reviews by men which foisted a Freudian and sexual theme on her work she responded, "Well, I made you take time to look at what I saw and when you took time to really notice my flower you hung all your own associations with flowers on my flower and you write about my flower as if I think and see what you think and see of the flower and I don't."

As Phil Leider taught us, we should "Trust the artist first." When we have not only the evidence of her life and work but the direct evidence of her comment on the very subject of Freudian/sexual interpretation, we ought to believe what the artist tells us.

Here is a quote from Sarah Greenough's essay "From The Faraway," which speaks to the early misguided criticism on O'Keeffe and which also brings to light the sexist nature of that criticism:

> The notoriety that O'Keeffe acquired in the 1920s, as a result of the large number of portraits Stieglitz made of her, significantly affected the critical reaction to her work. During this time, a large and very vocal majority of critics repeatedly discussed her painting in relation to her sex; they saw her first as a woman and only second, if at all, as an artist. Even in the early 1920s, when much of her work was quite abstract and devoid of sexual references, she was hailed as the "priestess of Eternal Woman." Readers were told that "the essence of very womanhood permeates her pictures." Lewis Mumford wrote, "She has beautified the sense of what it is to be a woman; she has revealed the intimacies of love's juncture with the purity and the absence of shame that lovers feel in their meeting." Freud's theories were extremely popular in the 1920s and undoubtedly encouraged sexual interpretations. Because she was so distressed by much of the critical writing about her, which was primarily by men, and because she hoped that another woman might see her art more clearly, she solicited reviews from several women. (pp. 136-7)

Greenough goes on to quote from reviews whose prose is even more purple than that above. I don't think that these early reviewers—or contemporary ones, for that matter—had to stay up very late to come up with the idea that there is something sexual about flowers; however, that was not why O'Keeffe painted them. Those were not her associations, and she said so. A portion of Juan Hamilton's essay "In O'Keeffe's World" from the same catalog of the retrospective show is a good counterpoint to the criticism of the 1920's and '30s:

> Her genius was her oneness with herself. Her ability to generate an aura of honesty and directness. There was a connection between her internal and external world that was full of truth. It appealed to a lot of people. So her flowers are flowers in their own way. They don't allude to other flowers. When she painted the West, it was the West she sensed. There is an openness in the pictures, and a magic sense of light. Other painters would come West and paint the hills of New Mexico in such a way that they looked like Connecticut. They would bring their own styles and assumptions and pin them on the work they did. She was an open person, open to new experience, in a fresh and honest way that was unique. (p.11.)

Still, some of that wrong-mindedness persists today. An example appeared in the Sept. 1989 issue of *Art & Antiques*. The magazine was previewing some of the paintings from the then new book of O'Keeffe paintings which would be released in time for Christmas, *Georgia O'Keeffe: In the West*. The issue featured an article by Hunter Drohojowska who was writing yet another biography on O'Keeffe for Knopf. Although it was otherwise an informative article, some very poor reasoning on pages 88 and 89 significantly damaged the essay. Commenting on some of the well known paintings of skulls and flowers, Drohojowska wrote:

> The surrealism of such paintings—with their ongoing theme of floating bones combined with landscape or flowers—is undeniable. O'Keeffe protested. "I was in the surrealist show when I'd never heard of surrealism. I don't think it matters what something comes from; it's what you do with it that counts. That's when it becomes yours." Of course O'Keeffe also claimed that her work had no sexual references, that it was all something made up by Stieglitz.

> Art Historians generally accept that an artist's own account of the genesis of his (her?) work must always be taken with a grain of salt. Witness Picasso's well-known claim that he had never seen an African mask when he painted the Demoiselles d'Avignon, contradicted by a photograph of the artist in his studio with just such a mask hanging on the wall.

Well, it's difficult to know where to begin with thinking this severely illogical. But, before I engage this quote line by line, I believe it is important to note that here again we encounter a fairly arrogant attitude. "As we all know," Drohojowska implies, "artists are not to be trusted." Just for the record and for common sense, I would venture that artists—if we want to risk sweeping such divergent personalities into a group—have as many honest, direct, or duplicitous members as any other "group"—say, academics, or art historians? Generalizing on this grand a scale leads to trouble—historically, racism and sexism, and, at the very least, inaccuracy. A case by case approach would seem to be the most accurate and profitable way to proceed in evaluation, especially when the writer / critic is writing a biography and ostensibly has some pertinent material from which to draw.

First of all, the tacit definition and application of Surrealism that Drohojowska offers here does not apply—bones combined with a desert landscape or flowers are not undeniably surrealist. There is no psychological atmosphere providing motivation and centering the emotion of the piece. Indeed, far from the images being juxtaposed, it is obvious that they are all from the same immediate environment. I would make the argument that some critics have made about De Chirico, that his work is not surrealist but rather still life taken off the table, an observation that seems more compelling for O'Keeffe than for De Chirico. Given the specific subjects O'Keeffe painted in the west, this seems fairly obvious, difficult to ignore, unless of course, your academic standing and/or writing career depended on manufacturing some new theory regardless of the evidence. Lacan has replaced Freud for this tenuous foothold and O'Keeffe and what she had to say about her style and her subject are conveniently put aside, for her own considerable writings about her work do not serve to advance the industry of academic speculation. There's not much profit for the writer to examine the art as art, its aesthetic goals and motivations. Painters, students of art would do so, but those more interested in advancing theory about work rather than the work itself, are, simply put, out to advance themselves and not the art.

In his essay "The Scholarship and the Life" in *From The Faraway Nearby*, (Ed.s. Merrill & Bradbury, Addison Wesley, 1992) James Craft, Assistant Director of the Whitney Museum, concludes by pointing to this trend in O'Keeffe criticism.

> One easily finds in O'Keeffe what one needs and then formulates her art and self to the shape of one's own vision. It is one of the exciting factors of her art and self that this happens, but it is a danger we must try to deal with as scholars and critics. (p. 27)

In the same book, art historian Anna C. Chave quite

logically exposes the bias, sexually and aesthetically, of the male critical response to O'Keeffe, especially early on. However, she then ignores O'Keeffe for her own interpretations, and while they are more feminist than masculine, they equally ignore O'Keeffe the artist and person, and this after she has stated that O'Keeffe knew what she was doing!

> But O'Keeffe was no plant, no amoeba, no dimwit: she was a self-possessed, literate person who formulated with great deliberateness often eloquent visual descriptions of her ideas, perceptions, and feelings. O'Keeffe saw art precisely as a means of saying what she wanted to say in a way that suited her.... Her art was prompted, then, by the realization that 'I was a very stupid fool not to at least paint as I wanted to and say what I wanted to when I painted....' (p.31)

Later in her essay, page 36, Chave finds it more profitable to disregard what O'Keeffe herself has said about her own art and substitute her, the critic/historian's, interpretation of the work, thinking, obviously, that she knows better than O'Keeffe: "O'Keeffe's objection to the sexual readings of her art probably had more to do with the degrading forms those readings took than with any naiveté about her works' sexual overtones."

It is hard to follow the thinking here. It is so facile to place a Freudian (all round shapes and spaces are feminist/feminine, womb-oriented) on to any art or objects. It seems to me an artist who wrote and talked as much about her work as O'Keeffe did, who lived a very long time and had ample opportunity to live through several decades and movements in art and in thought, and who said her considerations for style and subject were painterly ones, should be listened to. It seems presumptuous at best for historians and critics to assume they know better the intentions and achievements of the artist, but I have long been at odds with the theorists. Nevertheless, while there may be some room for interpreting an artist or writer who made no comment on his/her work or who is far removed in time, it makes no objective sense to disregard the expressed comment of a contemporary artist.

"Trust the artist first—not Johnny Carson, Dan Rather, not your parents, not art historians and academics—trust the artist." That is what one of the best teachers I ever had said to us. He was talking of Vermeer and Velasquez that day, showing us through the history of the artist's composition and body of work, how the artist was thinking when he made the work. Of course, there are many fine and helpful art historians who do somewhat the same thing, and it is granted that there have been artists who consciously or unconsciously mislead viewers, reviewers, interviewers, gallery owners. But when someone's life and writing is as direct and craft-oriented as O'Keeffe's, when her art and objects shine in such candid contexts, we ought to believe what she says. Moreover, if one were to err in believing the artist or the critic, I would vote for erring on the artist's side, for that would at least force us back to the work itself instead of some posturing and postulating about the work which is at least once removed from the process and the actual object.

The poems I wrote from the late '70s through the mid '80s based on O'Keeffe's paintings were published by Vanderbilt University Press in 1988— *Blossoms & Bones: On The Life and Work of Georgia O'Keeffe*. As I mentioned earlier, the monologue form immediately presented itself to me as I was so compelled by the images and also by her own voice in her writings. I was over-taken by the imagery and the life, and hence three of the poems in the book were even derived from some rather famous photographs of her. My attempt always was to stay close to a view, which, if she did not see it exactly that way, she would nevertheless find close to the mark.

In the early spring of 1990, three years later after I wrote the last poem that went into the Vanderbilt book, I had been looking at some of the paintings from that new book, *Georgia O'Keeffe: In The West*; I was especially taken with "Spring" and "The Beyond," her last painting. Along with the painting "Pelvis IV," they still held for me the wonder and mystery, the mystical assemblage and light that O'Keeffe's best work has always offered.

I thought about that for a few days while looking at the work, and one night just before sleep, that same voice entered my mind. I wrote down some notes for one poem and the next day drafted three poems; and when the poems came, they came in that quiet, meditative rush, just as if some voice were in fact entering me, or at least as if I were listening to some real voice. In the following weeks, I re-shaped them focusing on the idea and feeling of "last things" as seemed appropriate for "The Beyond," especially. I ended up revising the poems several times even after they were published. I tried to write some more on other paintings I had not considered, but the voice was gone.

It would be a number of years before I again heard that voice, lived with O'Keeffe's images, and found the words for that particular wondering about the earth and what might lie behind it, what glows within it. In 2000, I picked up the project again and had a group of fifteen new poems derived from O'Keeffe's western paintings. I submitted them to the Blue Light Press chapbook contest and was fortunate enough to have the ms. selected and published in 2001. I thought then that I had said all I had to say. Yet looking at the western paintings once again in 2003, the bones and flowers and vast desert spaces and sky suggested five more poems to me which I published with Cutaway Books in a letterpress limited edition. In working on this book, pulling together all 50 poems, I was given two last poems to close the collection. I trusted what the artist gave me, and remained as faithful as I knew how to what she saw.

I

BLOSSOMS & BONES:
On The Life and Work of Georgia O'keeffe

1.

Sky above Clouds

My first memory
is of the brightness of light—
light all around—
a quilt of it, a patchwork
of red and white blossoms on blue
like these clouds down the evening sky,
their form, their budding lines . . .

My mind holds them
stretching away
above the day's cadenza,
that half hour when the hills
glow and lift on a last held note—
it is then that my mind saunters
over the cool, immaculate squares
over the horizon line,
the next hill, where light flowers
across the finite trellis of this world . . .

Starlight Night

A life like any other on the plains,
and so I grew looking out to starlight
and the unknown, the scintillation
at the far string's end of my imagining.
I wished on the spangled fish and
kites of light and wanted to gather
these worlds the way I felt them there,
fasten them sparkling above the hum
and tug of this blue, blue heavy one.

And so each evening I set my heart
and eye seining among the thinning sky
and painted the budding schools of stars
with their rounded corners and irregular fix—
light has its forms, its violet madder,
but dreams vaguely by until we are pleased
with our own perceptions and see
its pulse backing the random void,
its puzzle locked in all we know.

But someone is always having a say
about how it should look, the wise men
disagreeing about stars and art, my art—
so many bickering crows of thought—
and finally, I am most interested
in what they don't say, because
there can be holes in the hard lines
of thinking, just as there are clear gaps
in this heaven's brilliant display. . .

Red Poppy

I want you to see
what I see of flowers—
the meaning of a word is not
the meaning of a color,
and so this scarlet poppy
doubled and redoubled
with its life, as flowers are relatively small
and no one has the time,
and seeing takes time.

There is no doubt here;
this effusive flower
draws us with a feeling
as direct as the sun, when,
as a child one bright-hot day,
I held my hand up
to shield my eyes and
saw my fingers glow
red as any flower or star
as the light seeped through them.

There is a dark abstraction
at the heart of it,
an intangible
that only comes clear in paint—
the colors in their lines
are often the most definite form
to say what I mean,
just as where I was born
and how I've lived do not,
when compared to what I've done.

What is of interest
is to love some small thing
and see how it grows within you,
how the petals,
the papery flesh of the flower,
barter with the wind
and carry life outward
as obviously as blood,
and not so unlike us.

Light Coming on the Plains

One long note's level drive
across the wash—we come in
at the crescendo, on the pollen
of light from the first idea
to fill space in a beautiful way.
In the spectrum's short waves
a blue concerto spins
a substance for the eye.

A dot, a water-splash,
and beneath the gas and custard light
something moves in what will be
a plain of amber waves,
a sea dark with breathing cells.

Each day we see the afterglow
singing over the earth's pale edge,
primordial as our blood, blue
and lightly swimming up our arms.

From this I learn the love
of paint as paint—the first life
coming into our eyes we can name
and tell things by, so we can worry
about the clothes we choose,
and how our hair goes grey.

from 10 Variations on the Evening Star in Daylight
(#s III, IV, V, VI)

I had nothing but to walk into nowhere
and the wide sunset space with the star—
far away from town it was high and bright
in the broad daylight.
                            Humming there
in the same key as the sun,
there was at first something prodigal
about it, but soon the sky toned out
and it was rare against the waves of light.

I was face to vast face
with my elements, one primary hand
of color like a fountain pushing up
the star—its yellow filaments
tinting green, the horizon red
and rolling as the day sank off
and somehow the sea, a long desert blue
in the absence of roads, fences, trees.

Once out here my sister
shot bottles thrown into the air—
now their white chits cannot be
found anywhere on the way home.

At this hour, the world is composed
of but a few basic lines,
and standing upright in the expanse,
I am only one more.

Palo Duro Canyon

Weather seemed to go over it,
wind and snow blew by the slit
in the plains as if it wasn't there.
We descended into that lone, dry place
down the cattle trails at evening;
the hills were sheer and
had a fiery, primeval film.

Even clouds hovered flame bright,
and far to the bottom
red rings of light,
perilous as the very place
Alighieri stood, or the dream
when your bed rises into the air
and you are about to fall . . .

We climbed out on all fours
and against the far sunset ridge
a long line of cattle headed down
like black lace on the canyon edge—
I kept my eye on a small wedge of blue
winging high and away.

Dead Cottonwood Tree, Abiquiu, New Mexico, 1943

The river has moved off somewhere
to sleep, singing to itself underground
past all these chartreuse sprigs and cholla,

and when it wakes must again shoulder
its own green weight in the world through
a distance of greasewood and iron-red hills.

But here, this tree is beyond all that, calm
as any bone or creekstone is calm—clearly
it has little more to do than let the sun

reminisce along this absent architecture
of limbs as they finger the abstract up-swing
of the blue, the watery applications of light.

Stripped down by air, remaindered to nothing
but the wind's thin arms, it's nevertheless turned
to it for solace, taken its wild grey notes to heart.

Train in the Desert—1916, charcoal on paper

And so it comes
shaving away the formless
dark with its dark form,
stripping the silence down
to a smoke of movement
pell mell down the iron
corridor of its two grey lines,
taking over this space
with the half-light
of some big idea
about ourselves,
as if we were sure
that this is progress
we've sent thundering
outward in circles of sound
for our own amazement,
as if we will matter
finally to the sand
and the sky's long view,
that haze traveling
continually about Time,
as if the hand of man
will outlast all this,
the world slipping darkly
off its wheels . . .

2

Summer Days / Ram's Head with Hollyhock

Because at first there were no flowers
I began picking up bones,
a place to begin to have a say.
They had nothing to do with death,
they outlasted it, and here, still
sparely support some long thinking.
We grow by pieces from what's around us;
these leftovers reaffirm our living
in the assonance of the space
they have let go.
               Wind-polished
and stubborn as the hills, the bones
share their distance washed away—
against the cloud-sweep a skull
is eloquent as a single hollyhock.
Red salvia and sunflower, violet daisy,
were raised by rivulets of wind
and then remembered by red hills,
the very earth ground petal by petal
to powder and mixed to paint them.
A ram's head, a deer's head,
are the final flowers
in relation to the sky,
and please me very much—
they are resplendent
and sing in their own right
like summer days always coming back
to the storm-blue matter of the mind.

Flowers and clouds go up, so much
smoke in the heat, tossed,
chaff as the body is chaff;
and only the shale of bones
offers a reply.
                    Still, bones
have something for us;
they come back, shapes in our mind
better than flowers, but flowers
nonetheless—the pure sun-white bloom
we all have in us, living, and after.

Ladder to the Moon

Stopped short on a dark earth
each day, there is more left to do.
Like the ragged peaks of the Pedernal,
I reach and have patience,
the good roof of my will,
against the unvaried clouds of dust.
I take hold of whatever comes along—
horse skull, pelvis, shell—
to say what is to me the shape
of wonder, the wideness of it here.

Half a moon hangs high and white,
blossom or hull beyond your feet?
Always something glimmering above you
and how to touch it to be sure?

You must become fluent with your hands,
make something of the sky's blue-green
nettle, the invisible bones
that get us from heart to mind.
There is a fitness of things, and,
as I see it, a lean body on two good arms,
and tonight this ladder for the moon—
this pure saddle of light floating
down a breath-thin line
as night by sleeping night
you climb out of this life
as sure as you stand here, longing.

Black Cross, New Mexico

Black, a cross blocks out
the blue and ash-like
lift of evening—only
a far dot of moon rises
freely, white and wafer-thin.
And you will come upon
a cross almost anywhere here,
appropriate to these hills
which are as evenly shaped
as souls, edged blue-grey
and bright as embers
while the flat flame
of the horizon holds.

The cross is broad, strong,
driven together by four pegs;
it divides east and west—
on the one hand the dust,
on the other the dark.
Painting it is a way
of painting this country
as I felt it
in its penitent glow—
but burnt or burning,
it's long been too late
to save this land
for anything except
what's left of the light.

Two Jimson Weeds

Self-assured as clouds
they bloom and come on
at evening in the cool.
Beneath the moon
the sweet fragrance
calls you from the house
to take the air
like a sherbet after meals.
Hearts of pale Mars violet,
of light lime green, and
the feeling you could swim in.

Long veins hold the flower
open to look at you,
but I found they are the death
of horses and persist back
through the bones and sand.
Yaquis have some use of them,
another fear half-known.

But I paint these flowers
with nothing more behind them
than sky on rising sky,
equivalent of the sigh I felt—
I have only to think
of their delicate colognes
to feel the coolness
of evening pass over me.

A Black Bird with Snow-covered Hills /
Black Bird Series (In the Patio IX)

I would have it seen
this common feat of a blackbird's flight,
(always there, always going away)
because much is hidden from us
as our heads start to circle
with sleep and the desire in the world,
like these clay-red hills covered with snow
over which the dark birds veer.

Those who lie late in dreams
calling lowly, *let me be,*
wake to this agent of the close-at-hand
when he's an omen on the porch,
their spirit's knife to divide them
breast from wing, bait for the blue.

A crow's riff above the hills
comes back from the cave,
from the mind's one angle—
hard, darted lines
high above the limbs of the cold.

And so I shape what I can,
bend the objective feathers to fit
the abstract and brief term
of beauty, reminding us
of our feet midway in an old road—
this way but once, and we pass.

Black Hills and Cedar

All on their own
             the black hills come up
                          and the clouds,
bone-pure, just over them—
                    humped, dark as two brick ovens,
then that line of white, like a compromise.

I like it here
             as nothing is completely desolate
unto itself,
             lost as light out here might be
in its charcoal and flesh-full strains
                                if no one
rode out to see it.

                    Always in this wind-bare gulch,
some small thistle
                    will pull blood out.
This cedar bush for instance—
                          creviced in
the wash and cutaways
                    of the hills' burnt skin,
bottomed-out
             where the sand backs up—
                                is just now
flourishing, funneling in the cloud
                          and run offs,
shooting out boughs
                    the salty green of sea waves
blown back,
             the dappled blooms outdone
only by the distance of the blue.

Ansel Adam's Photo, "Georgia O'Keeffe and Orville Cox, Canyon de Chelly National Monument 1937"

Surrounded by so little
we were unmindful as the clouds
sifting into that long wash,
that slow cut of time, as it sloughed
another of its half-bright skins.
You buttoned your jacket and leaned into the wind,
my pale wrist was a flower there, bent
toward you and the unassuming skies.

And so our plain features
just fell into agreement
with a fading world of clouds—
and behind us, the ghost riders,
our hearts' white horses turning grey.

The West has almost disappeared except
in films where cowboys in black & white
are as humble in their hats as we
before a far and still horizon.

And given these long ropes of clouds,
their knots of loss largely overlooked,
this might well be all of this earth
we'll recall before we're ridden out
on the spare and uncoaxed focus of the light.

3

The New York Paintings

Even now it's like a dream,
the city going up
like tall thin bottles
with fluttering moths of light,
dark even by day as the towers
pinch out the sky and ice-blue
glass centers down their brick.
The grand height of all of it
kept me painting, looking up
to the perfect rise and rub of blocks,
the spangled avenues by night
in a line off toward the stars,
intersections where sky boxed through
with the unexpected sun biting
a piece out of the Shelton,
and sun spots stalling in the shafts of air.

But this passes in the paint
like dust dissolving red as a stop light,
red as the East River under the burning stacks.
Soon the sounds of traffic and harbor boats
are long and sad as lowing cattle
and finally you feel raw
beneath these high-toned stars,
feel hunted by the buildings
angled over you like hawks.

Lurking on a ridge of clouds and smoke
there's a Billy-the-Kid moon,
and you find yourself turning in the dark
toward the sudden snap of a match
and asking *¿Quien es?*

59th Street Studio

With a northern skylight
and two windows to the south,
with pale lemon walls
and an orange floor,
this loaned space was not
what you dream of for painting.

I chose instead
the room back of the studio,
the narrow window opening
onto a small court—I chose
the beige and light blue of evening
moving through it, the stone-blank
outer walls, the terra rosa
of the sunset and smoke
edging through the glass,
a last white wing
above it all.
Without bombast
or bright gates thrown open
we should discover our place
subtly, and by degree trim
the dark from the simple medium
our hearts should be, so
the little we have to say or see
resonates, and bears us up.

East River No. I

Dead of winter and nothing
visible on the opposite bank
but those black stacks towering
their throaty smoke and turning
to frost against the lifeless grey,
the blur and shroud of December.
As far as I can see
this could be the city
of the dead, shades stalled
among some dimmer shades.
Even on the near shore
the ramparts of roaring
industry are stopped, black
and bloodless as the bricks,
as the roads going nowhere fast.

And several stories above it all
I think that if there are two worlds
there is little difference between them
now—the cold thickens everything,
the roots of ice break up the streets,
and no one will be buried today,
no one ferried to the other side.

Confined to my apartment, I manage
with the little glow seeping in
beneath the level of the clouds,
the steam heat and blank length
of room, this time on my hands
and the little life I rub into them
before starting back to work
and looking down the dreary air

to where the smoke's brief light
touches off an ice-white swath
of water, as I take my sweater's
arm and wipe the window clear.

Lake George with Crows / Black Hollyhock, Blue Larkspur / The Lawrence Tree

Summer in Taos.
On a bench beneath the big tree
on the Lawrence ranch,
I'd drift a bit toward sleep,
toward the past in colors—
trunk and branches of the tree
in a heart-tangle
toward whatever's backing stars,
bark and leaves red/black
as hollyhock, the sky blooming
blue as larkspur I found
in an open field nearby.

Overall, the indigo of dream,
and I'd see Lake George, poplars
tall and breathing to maroon hills,
cloud-streak silvered with moon,
and a birch shimmering at the edge—
golden leaves I'd row myself beneath
admiring the many choices
upper branches made for the sky.
Over the cerulean lake, three crows
tilted like dim ideas of myself
as I felt the flower-cool air
in either hand and in my face
and was of three minds,
flying equally off—

do I break for the far beyond,
or fall back slowly
to the bench and grey earth, or
hover a while in between,
dipping wings to the mirror
and calling for the firmament to see
how the powdered light spreads
before the blank dimension of dawn?

Pelvis and Moon / Pelvis III / Cow's Skull—Red, White and Blue

These are what is left for our imagining—
husks we can hold out against the sky
and let our eye sing through for shape
when there's more sky than earth to deal with.
These bones were useful as any heart,
and now, held rightly to the air, are wings
to keep our vision poised.
                              You look through
holes to a blue that outlives us all
and see how the white curves keep us.
And below a chalk-dust midday moon,
staring there like any cow skull
you come on face to face, you find
that the light pours through each way.

As the sea comes back here, your hands
turn cold holding these hip bones up;
as the sage in wind laps like waves on a shore,
as some mussels turned a million years to stone
still offer a bit of their original blue,
your arms raise these spirits' staves
shining with use like your own, before they too
are left somewhere dully in a sandy unknown.

From the White Place

Whatever brings us out of this
bottom rock and sun-drowned daze,
out of this hollow gorge,
this boneyard, these broken trails
we walk looking down for stones,
for deadwood, the dying in our way?

I often content myself
with these ivory pillars, this limestone
unfolded and thumbed upwards
by the ghost of lost water,
layered as salts or silts are,
like time calcified, like thick
petals of a calico rose,
like slowed clouds—shimmied up
by wind to where a patch of green
breathes out over the headland's crest.

At dawn or late at evening, the sky
too is white above here, a muslin sheet
calm beyond the turquoise or amethyst air.
I come here to be reminded
from the umber and the gold,
from the land's dramatic gestures
as it breaks itself down,
how pure the palette can finally be—
these few columns, rinsed with sun,
lift me—mountain's husk like chalk,
like snow, like our last words
up this dry waterfall of light.

Road Past the View

From my window
on the expanse,
the road goes out
a silver blue, a vein
dying flame-like for Santa Fe.
It makes a wide smooth sweep
loving the hills, the sand
handwritten with sun.
Past the trees and mesa
which do not count for much
in the eye's long run,
it almost stands up in air
and breaks cleanly
toward the peaks
of the Sangre de Cristo
powdered with that distant
and imagined light.
The road points finally
high and to the left,
some other corner of the earth,
but slides back easily
in the sharp angle of my thought,
saying always its little bit
about roads, how the shape
and direction of things assist
the heart, and are vital signs
by which we reach for what
is just beyond our view.

4

Shell I

I picked it up in the Yucatan
beached in the undergrowth where
tides rinse themselves of life—
bleached earring of light,
even now when I hold it up
the sea comes back to me
with what we know and don't know.

Each shell is a world in itself
and looking closely from the side
it is impossible to tell
whether it winds inward,
shaded heart-wise toward itself,
or outward spinning off its last
rough flakes of time.

Like this shell resting on dark glass,
like the red coral left on the sand,
what we've touched and taken in,
what calls us back, tells us how,
chamber upon chamber, our years
add their beauty and regret
until our bones break open
and we are salt flowers, star floss,
luminous shapes for wind, outlines
on the narrow isthmus of the soul.

Ranchos Church No. 1

The nave billowing
like the arched
backbone of a cloud,
two L-shaped wings
and the way they sidle
up to air—each dune-
like slope of wall hard
with that dark movement
skirting the evening
mountain's edge as it
persists before the flat
abstraction, the eternal
attrition of that blue.

These forms withstand
the steady re-thinking
of the wind, the old
indifferences of earth.
And somehow this thick
clay supports the heart,
takes us gradually up
level upon level above
the dust, the sky's sand
and streaks of loss.
    And here,
stepping out one day
we might take our place
just outside the anonymous
flags of clouds, the incidents
of our lives then amounting
to little more than the uneven
but sturdy praise of our hands,
these worn but undiminished
aspirations of line to light.

Black Cross with Stars and Blue

The evening gives way
to the gleaming concourse
of other worlds—the near planets
and undistanced stars swim
up the dark and pause.

And looking up,
we secretly call out
to four or five
wishing with an absent mind,
supposing an unfettered drifting off.

But this is a parochial place
where mountains halt
before the azure reach
of sky or thought, where our feet
bring us to conjecture
among the sand and sagging bones
of earth.
        Clearly, this life is
staked to the body and
these dark markers remind us
of all that's driven through
the simple fiber of our desire.

And although we've seen the earth
as one bright mote blown
across the splintery plains of space,
all our stars, and so much blue,
still cross our hearts.

Philippe Halsman's Photo of Georgia O'Keeffe at Abiquiu, New Mexico, 1948

This is what I have—a ghosted adobe ranch,
ironwood and mesquite, the smoke tree's buds
with their blue apology to heaven—the desert
in its every part saying *loss,* and then
these clouds shaping and reshaping the days
to say that loss and gain are nothing,
that flowers and bone are much the same,
that I'm welcome to whatever I find.

Rivers and an unseen shore, clouds hold over us
that first enigma—the soul's white dust set against
our affinity for form, against the wind, and always
we are asked to step out of our dark coat and hat,
out of the little space that is the very earth,
in our last shirt formless as the flagstone
scattered across this yard, as these clouds thinning
like the end of all desires, and reminding us
that there are things we will never know.

Despite them, I know some small thing—
you choose a place and begin to work;
the sun divides everything into equal parts
and you adjust your eye, your heart,
and, one more piece of this light,
praise these bright, diminished reaches.

Or you come upon a cattle skull, its jaw
a lock of time turned skyward in the old silence—
still, your fingers sidle up to the blind eye and
bad teeth, and with a white scarf about your head,
with the simple language of sand, you start
to understand the dry blossom we are all becoming.

I have a ladder set to my roof from where
I can paint the moon, that dreamer's stone,
bone to bone as resourcefully as the clouds
or jimson weeds, as sparely as the clock of stars.
God, I suppose, leaves us to our own designs
until we too are only remnants of this place.

Red Hills and the Sun, Lake George

Before the birds' aubade
or the milky rose of mist
tips skyward off the surface
of the lake, before you think
to speak, the white center,
the bare bone of light,
loosens itself in aqua
and violet arcs above
the swales and folds
of hills whose wind-cut lines
shrug off the dark in perfect
memory of themselves .

I like this first hour,
the glissandi of sunlight
ringing between the sky
and a land whose skin
is the wind-burnt color
of pomegranates flayed
and vibrant in the frost.
And of all there is
this might be enough
to choose from, were we ever
again to say how we'd have
the world, see it made over
in an image all its own.
For now, these hills lift
like hands—implicit
in their praise of nothing
more than earth and air,
and so remind me that
longing and acceptance
are equal parts of prayer.

Shell and Old Shingle VII
(mountain across the lake)

Today, I'm of a different mind,
nothing lives in me
with a bright, hard line,
and what I feel is so faint
that the red day's threads
are washed-out mauve in a cloud
that this grey lake mirrors.
I find I've painted my life,
things happening in my life,
without knowing it until now,
until this view from the window
onto these shells and crusts
floating at my arms' length.

The mountain's a weatherbeaten shingle,
one flap of a heart purely penitent
in this bruised hour, this amethyst light—
I think of doves, of ash,
and the coarse shirts of saints,
of how smoke gives ground and kisses
before it dies skyward, paler
than our life as we are losing it...
This is a last blush, the rose of dust
on our cheek and soft upturned palms.
These are the last shades of evening
and in them you want to breathe out
with everything you have
and hold on to the burning.

Red Hills and Bones

No one takes the absence
into account the way I do—
this rind of backbone, the bridge
and scale of its blank articulation,
sustains some perfectly whole
notes of light against the raw
muscle of the land unbound,
the undercurrents surfacing
in concert with the white riffs
of cholla spotting the swales.

Put right, one part of loss
counterpoints the next, leaves us
much to see despite the frank
abrasion of the air. Finally,
this thighbone is every bit
the bright, hard stuff of stars
and against the hills'
rust and clay sets free
a full, long silence here
that as much as anything
sings all my life to me.

Juan Hamilton's Black & White Photo on the Back of the Penguin Edition of the Paintings

Can this be the earth?
I answer directly as the eye serves
tied to the form of things
summer in the mind...
My world was not all here before
I shaped it, pared it
subtly as a cloud does,
bringing weather, suggesting to wind,
moving bracelets of sand here,
raising the hills' red hands there,
accepting the world insofar
as a cloud accepts light
passing through it...

And so I am here,
available to the distance,
and have settled with the rain
that cuts its place and fires
the saguaro seed to reach
and hold its own, bloom forcefully
for the sun.
I offer this land
in its hearted shades,
the wearing down of things
against their own life,
that you might see how
the honing, the spareness
of their essential light
is that beauty we are
always looking toward.

The evening calls such a song
after a long walk to a knoll
from which we can see best.
We stand here and prepare,
staring flatly out at a future
where our bones will fall or rise
behind us like any fish or flower
and our souls fly out
like fireflies to the night.
My star-white bolt of hair unwinds
toward the deep rose of space,
its spinning rinds,
and what shells beach up from this
hard-hewn body's shore, say
I made this, lived here, and more.

II

Against the Blue

1

Spring, 1948

What to tell you now
                    Of everything
I've come to here?
                    First and last I am
Given to this light,
                    Its scenarios and silver wash
Pulled down and
                  Threaded among the fabrics of Spring—
Then the sky
      Which frames my thinking like water settled
Through sand,
                And air that has backbones breaking
                      away in their lines
Like wings
      Left over from another life . . . .
                    But I'm not here to argue
Against the blue, that usual view of time
                Riding the flat distance out, light-
Less and far beyond the Pedernal.
          I only have the pilgrim's burning hope
Which carries me year to year
      Until I stand in the consuming sun with images
Of a world re-made
      Whirling through my hands again, and the
                    day-mists lifting
All this space
      In its weightlessness—in its high, white,
                  primrose bloom . . . .

Red Hills with White Cloud

Outside my door
even the grass is gone,
the earth rolling away
to rust beneath the blue . . . .

I am left with just these
red hills to take to heart—
hills which will out-live
my eyes, their ruts and
grooves where rain
uncovered the even
cadences of clay, where
wind eliminated all allegory
from the land.
          There is
only one spun-cloud smudge,
one scumbled image
to suggest the ghost ship
of my mind, one something
above perspective that I have
no name for beyond breath,
beyond a vista surviving
with these values of blood . . . .

Blue River—Chama River, Ghost Ranch

It's today, 1935,
and the grey
as cardboard clouds
have slipped off east,
and a friend from Chicago
has driven me out
to catch the bands
of spring pushing through,
bright along the hills
despite the pink sandy ruts
and fossil white banks,
the ghostly dust.
Hard and soft greens,
the cottonwoods
and mesquite, some dots
of pine starting back—
they all know the river
swirling out again,
light blue as my old
work shirt hung
on a windy line
against the hills,
the shirt I wear painting
so I am not here
more than the water—
all this Time disappeared
in these blue turns
flowing upwards,
like a sky.

for Jean Armstrong Corle

Rust Red Hills

I don't know
what you might be
thinking, what you might
bring to this, here
among the hills—
but I see no need
for the scholars of dust
and shade to pronounce
on the manifest bones
of the earth as I have
found them, polished
and attended by light.

Miles of badlands, but
all the colors of my palette
emerge like old Spanish coins
working up through sand,
five degrees of rust—
copper, and gold sparks to
red-hot iron and black, and
one ribbon of deep ocean
green on old brass—
set across the clay,
the sediments and
the imagination, as obvious
as flowers elsewhere.
These tap my heart,
and my habit of mind fixes
a place for them beneath
the sky, where a pair of clouds,
thin as angels' wings, over-
looks it all.

I have hidden
nothing in these shapes
as there was nothing
to hide in the first place—
just this place that needed
no one to make more of it
than the unavoidable
tumbled shapes left shining
for us to understand . . . .

Who would I be
if I said these burls
of rock and clay stood
for some meaning outside
of themselves? The living
and the dead come to this,
which is neither,
and also more . . . .

White Place In Shadow

These pillars
to the sky
where the days
burn out white
dust in the west
and dissolve.

Some shadow
here over
the continuing
aspirations
of the earth,
a little ash
of light sifted
down from
the thin sky,
cool and water-
colored where
the wind goes
through this V
in the columned
stone—passage
from world
to world . . . .

2

Hills and Mesa To The West

I come this way
for the sun, set
on the far, dark
table of the west
where the evening
invites us to admire
the spare outbursts
of juniper and piñon
climbing out of canyons
and the wash—green
and gold remains
from the dry, com-
pounded heart of the sea
that moved off
in search of itself
before we were here
to know anything
was missing.
         It left
the blunt bones
of the land, and time
trailing off in the specks
of sand, in the one
essential embrace
of light anodized
high on the peak
of this brick-red
hill, and—as far
as I can see—made for
no purpose beyond this.

Pelvis IV, (Oval With Moon)

Close up,
far Away,
what could be
clearer than this
equivalency
of earth to sky—
brace that held
something heavy up,
now a flower-white
form for air, a stem
with the watery petals
of the sky working
through?
           And these
shapes let us slip
away—two-toned
and half-absent with
the light of the earth
released and yet over-
whelming in our bones.

When dreaming
off into space
sometimes,
I can put it right—
allow my thoughts
to be airborne
like the opaque
layers of the soul,
circle upon circle,
or a circle within
which plays-out

at arms' length, and
is also breathtaking—
as for example,
this smoke-colored moon
the blue takes in
with its thin recoveries
and light-full
circle of loss.

Flying Backbone

See how we are bound
    here a while
In the sea-deep alloy
    of sand and
Oxygen—our selves water-
    heavy and
Low, lusterless as river
    bottom clay.

In us, the invisible ladder
    of our bones
Skimming the surface for
    so long until
One twilight, all color is drown
    in the susurration
Of the sky, and thistle-like
    we are unknotted—
Arms white and wide for
    the ascending air. . . .

Pelvis With The Distance

Little finally
separates us
from the dish rag
sky, which is all
that might remain
of us past
a polonaise
of clouds

even as these
light-bleached staves
cut sharply
to the center
of something
as free from
Time as the colorless
haze always at
the lost horizon.

Relic, polished
with the litanies
of wind, this saddle
of old light
admits its absence—
a small round star,
portal, last vowel
for all our longing
to touch things,
to be in this world
if only to sing
mutely as the dust
through the air
without us.

Hernandez Church, New Mexico

This too, just bones—
just the pale earth pushed up
in the shape of Hope, perhaps—
holding off the grey weight of a sky
the size of God's fist.

These slabs, stripped down,
dulled with gusts, are no more
than the thigh bone or rib
I bring back from the badlands
and hold against the blue to see
what is left to praise,
what flat relics still resonate
beyond everything we know
of vast and unknowable space—
what essential notes might sing
through the walls, untouchable
as the one small source of light . . . .

3

Black Place Painted Grey

Now I think I know
This about the past . . .
Like an old negative
Where everyone we've lost
Walks in dim relief—
And perhaps in this
It is not so different
From what is to come?

Here where the sea
Is gone five million years
To bone-grit and salt,
Where molecules have come
To their small collective
Grief—this lost and almost
Neutral place
                    Where a grey
Wave of bare hills
Walls-up and tumbles
Down
          Above a tide
Of white wind
Which, in its spindrift
And brilliant throes,
Knows the calcium
Of regret—the cloud
Before us, above us,
Ice-blue.

Red Hills With Pedernal, White Clouds

I never wanted all that much
And so I found it—skinned land exposed,
Countless lesions in the sun, a few
Sticks of cedar trees, flesh-red
Rocks, the irresolute hills.

Then the inevitable bones scattered
Like light between the long shadows
And watery dark spaces—no promises there,
Our hopes opaque as the dusk-worn base
Of the Pedernal, shining above a life.

At sunset, an anaphora of western clouds,
White kites carried off with some last
Prayers written there on the loose
Meters of the air—
        The invisible
Strings in our hands, finally, pulling us
Toward God, or the stars, beyond everything
We know.
        Here, I know the cold
Night's hands in my star-colored hair
As I keep a firm grip on each thing
Not yet lost in the arms of the wind—
There is still a little light over the mountain,
Like a hand waving in the distance.

Datura and Pedernal

Here, when I close my eyes, I see the pure
    Symmetry of petals, the closed

Universe open in my mind across the desert's
    Unbending space, above

The suffering and sand blasted hills, skin-
    Toned and living in their way.

I am mid air with the flower, the far flat peak
    Of the Pedernal an alter to the blue

Where the landscape has been left behind
    In the backwash of wind. I have

The five points of its round, immaculate face
    Before me, life-sized before everything

In the reduced distance. Stainless as starlight,
    It is its own source, spinning away

Toward the green wick at the center, toward
    The unburdened mind's horizon,

The one round achromatic first word, sound
    In starry Sanskrit saying White

As it dreams over this world a while. Who
    Would say this is the image

Of the soul and not the absolute flower
    Itself, in its primordial, egg-

White spark—yet perhaps what the soul was,
    Before the soul was ours?

Above Clouds Again

Last light barring the bright
Edge of the world, at the end
Of all the suppositional
Umber and russet bits below—
All of it, nevertheless, going
Somewhere, with or without me
And every earth-ground
Ivory or amber shard
I held up to that glow,
Gone west with everything
I had to give.
        What spare beauty
In those bones, in the clouds,
What assurance and self possession
Moving over the sands—
             I covered all
I could before I came to the silt
And half luminous chalk,
The last mist the soul becomes
Unmitigated by the neutral
Avenues of air . . . .

The Beyond (Last, Unfinished Painting)

I rarely paint anything I don't know very well. And now
nothing has come to me more simply—just as when I've
been flying, time and history straighten out and fade into
the flat edge of the planet below. Any time I'm up there,
it's a study of basic things: the rim of space squaring-
off absolutely above the earth which is black, which
I'm finally done with, and which I'm content to leave as
pure abstraction as it may have always been. There's
the sky-window blue beyond, swirl and sea-colored
residue of our thought risen bright and breathing, then
a darker hue. A cold light skims the middle ground to
a vanishing point I once would have given its fiery due,
a blood-tincture, but now know better. A horizon, bone
clear, cuts through and is left unfinished, and comes as
close to what I wanted to say about all this anyway.

III

The Sudden Sky

From The Plains I

I think I have it now—
whipsaw arcs of dust
summer-long
across the sun,
drawing up the level
bounty of the land.
If someone went beyond
the wind storms and
wheat-thick daze,
indefinite at the center
of the air, attached
to everything we were
left to tend,
she might look up,
like me, and wonder . . . .
It was not for me—
it was a good place
to be from—a baseline,
and steady pulse
behind you,
a red getaway to
the sudden sky.

Pelvis with Shadows and the Moon

At night
        the deep river
                rises
floating
        the flower-shaped
                fragments
of dreams
        the subliminal
                loops and holes
through which
        our loosened shapes
                escape
the weight of sand
        and the dark
                implications
of the earth
        bound and
                water-heavy
with hope
        of something
                to be retrieved
or yet to come
        bleached
                or midnight blue
such husks
        recast
                the fear
the fierce riders
        of wind
                and yet suggest
forms
        unknotted
                from the frame
the bone white hole
        a moon
                will never fill.

White Sweet Peas

Air from cloud to cloud—
white taffeta, flat
and refolded
on the swept curves,
climbing for the breathing
blue, the sun-strong stem.
Such flourishes
and faultless switch-
backs involved
just over the green,
invisible edge
of spring—a lavender
ash of days
scumbling along
the chalk-thick ruffles,
re-establishing their
time signatures
above the ground:
these layers, the un-
complicated color
and scale of thought . . . .

Memory—Late Autumn

Still in October
as the amber
fog, the past
half shimmers
in its veil of rust—
dull fire burnished
at several removes
beyond the heart . . .
everything we know
behind us, yet
it ticks here
like low flames,
like the leaves
that just moments ago,
were here . . . .
All this smoke
through the mind's
dim branches again,
bright, for a while,
as the evening star . . . .

On the Old Santa Fe Road

Anymore, you see
next to nothing
from here—
just one wing
of sky brazing
the foothills like
the blue tips of flame. . . .
But I'm interested
in how this stretch
made out, abandoned
to the hard
hands of the wind,
the arbitrary
shifts in view,
those ten thousand
fine points that dissolved
like haze and left you
with your one life . . . .

Someone drove all night
to get here once
and then was gone
in time, and from
your front porch
you became acquainted
with the intrigue
of the stars . . . . Now
these calluses of sun,
these bald and unrelieved
remains. What ever was
lost, you can find
a trace of it here
if you look hard enough.

In any direction,
it's just a matter of dust,
before we come back
to this old lost way . . . .

IV
2007

On Georgia O'Keeffe's
"From The Faraway Nearby"

One wondered at first—
no rain, flowers didn't come.
But bones everywhere,
the parched light
of far hills,
their difficulty, steep,
only a place or two to climb
down or up.
          But then
you go on day long
with life's long project
of longing, picking up
the random sticks,
the scattered bits
of thought—beyond Fear,
the pink mist of it,
the white dust
hovering above those hills
where it's been kept
at arm's length, extended
beneath a comforting blue,
which, even in a painting,
is a concept with limitations,
which cannot forever
be the case . . . .
           Finally,
the most fearsome
of the abandoned skulls,
polished with the invisible
grit of wind,
held at close range,
gives back our flat

abstract reflections—
no turning away.
Significant, insignificant,
I have been of both minds
given the line of sight
available from here.
The hills seem small
because the place
they are washing away to
is so wide—
the air barely
carrying the indisputable
report of how
quick and close
this breathless distance
has always been . . . .

"That memory or dream thing I do . . ."
— Pedernal, 1945

Outside my window
the breeze in the piñon tree
tells me about the shape
of weather and other things
I love in space.
          That
Pedernal is a platform
for the blue, where
I send my greetings
to the sky, and go
when ever I can,
wondering if one side
alone could be
big enough
to see past the dry
never-ending
land?
    There is
a natural music
in the wind
which loops back
from abstraction to
the root of the tree,
consonant with bones,
the sand sifting
to start over
out there.
        I have to
get along with myself
the best way I can
if I am going to be
lifted past the vast

dust of starlight,
the indelible
core below the ridge
on my unconscious,
beyond which
I will not
compromise . . . .

About Christopher Buckley

Christopher Buckley's most recent books are *AND THE SEA*, (2006), and *SKY* (2004) from The Sheep Meadow Press.

His 16th book of poetry, *MODERN HISTORY: Prose Poems 1987-2007*, will be published by Tupelo Press in September 2008. *ROLLING THE BONES* will appear from Eastern Washington Univ. Press in early 2009.

With Gary Young Buckley is the editor of *The Geography of Home: California's Poetry of Place* (1999), and with David Oliveira and M.L. Williams he is editor of *How Much Earth: The Fresno Poets* (2001). For the Univ. of Michigan Press' Under Discussion series, he has edited *The Poetry of Philip Levine: Stranger To Nothing*, 1991.

Recently he has edited the poetry anthology, *Homage To Vallejo*, Greenhouse Review Press, 2006. And, with Alexander Long, *A CONDITION OF THE SPIRIT: THE LIFE AND WORK OF LARRY LEVIS*, Eastern Washington Univ. Press, 2004.

BEAR FLAG REPUBLIC: Prose Poems & Poetics from California, edited with Gary Young, is just out from Alcatraz Editions.

Over the last 30 years his poetry has appeared in *APR, POETRY, FIELD, The Georgia Review, The Iowa Review, TriQuarterly, The Kenyon Review, Ploughshares, The New Yorker, The Nation, The Hudson Review, The Gettysburg Review, Quarterly West, Prairie Schooner, & New Letters* among others.

He has received a Fulbright Award in Creative Writing to the former Yugoslavia, four Pushcart Prizes, two awards from the Poetry Society of America, and is the recipient of NEA grants in poetry for 2001 and 1984. Recent poetry awards include the City Works National Writers Award for 2006 from San Diego Community College, and the Kenneth O. Hansen poetry award from HUBBUB magazine.

He is a Guggenheim Fellow in Poetry for 2007-2008., and teaches in the creative writing Program at the Univ. of California Riverside.

Printed in the United States
201606BV00003B/1-156/P

9 781421 898483